Pebble® Plus

Weather Basics

Wind

by Erin Edison

Consulting Editor: Gail Saunders-Smith, PhD

CAPSTONE PRESS
a capstone imprint

Pebble Plus is published by Capstone Press,
151 Good Counsel Drive, P.O. Box 669, Mankato, Minnesota 56002.
www.capstonepub.com

 Books published by Capstone Press are manufactured with paper
containing at least 10 percent post-consumer waste.

Library of Congress Cataloging-in-Publication Data
Edison, Erin.
 Wind / by Erin Edison.
  p. cm.—(Pebble plus. Weather basics)
 Summary: "Simple text and full-color photographs describe wind and how it affects weather"—Provided by publisher.
 Includes bibliographical references and index.
 ISBN 978-1-4296-6054-9 (library binding)
 ISBN 978-1-4296-7082-1 (paperback)
 1. Winds—Juvenile literature. I. Title. II. Series.
 QC931.4.E35 2012
 551.51'8—dc22   2010053974

Editorial Credits
Erika L. Shores, editor; Kyle Grenz, designer; Laura Manthe, production specialist

Photo Credits
Image courtesy of Earth Sciences and Image Analysis Laboratory, NASA Johnson Space Center, 13
Shutterstock: Darren Baker, 5, David Steele, 21, George Bailey, 15, Gregory Johnston, back cover, JOANCHANG,
    cover, Marty Ellis, 19, Peter Wey, 9, Petronilo G. Dangoy Jr., 7, Poznyakov, 1, Ramon Berk, 17, Zastol`skiy Victor
    Leonidovich, 11

Artistic Effects
Shutterstock: marcus55

**Capstone Press thanks Mike Shores, earth science teacher at RBA Public Charter School
    in Mankato, Minnesota, for his assistance on this book.**

Note to Parents and Teachers

The Weather Basics series supports national science standards related to earth science. This
book describes and illustrates wind. The images support early readers in understanding the
text. The repetition of words and phrases helps early readers learn new words. This book
also introduces early readers to subject-specific vocabulary words, which are defined in the
Glossary section. Early readers may need assistance to read some words and to use the Table of
Contents, Glossary, Read More, Internet Sites, and Index sections of the book.

Printed in the United States of America in North Mankato, Minnesota.
032011   006110CGF11

Table of Contents

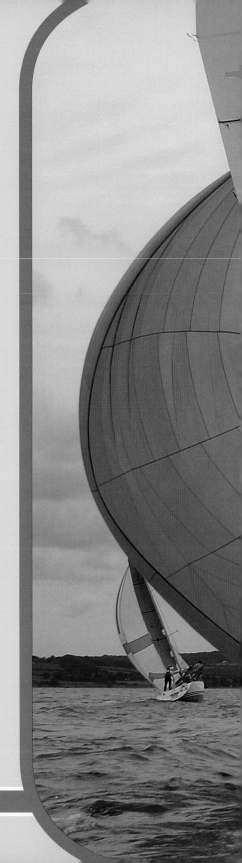

What Is Wind?

What pushes sailboats

across the water?

What rustles tree leaves?

It's moving air, called wind.

Sunlight warms air unevenly.

Cool air sinks. Warm air rises.

These air movements are wind.

Wind and Weather

Wind affects the weather.

It moves rain clouds.

Rain falls on the land

and water below.

9

Tornadoes and hurricanes are

storms with extreme winds.

These storms cause

major damage.

tornado

Kinds of Wind

Global winds blow air over large parts of Earth. Jet streams are long ribbons of powerful global winds. Storms follow paths made by jet streams.

jet stream

13

Local winds blow only

short distances.

Winds that move kites and

toss leaves are local winds.

A light local wind is a breeze.

It moves grass. A very strong

local wind is a gale.

Gales bend trees

and break branches.

We Need the Wind

Wind helps plants and animals. Birds fly faster and farther because of wind. Wind carries seeds and pollen.

People use wind turbines
to catch wind. The wind turns
blades to make electricity.
Wind turbines help people
use the power of wind.

Glossary

breeze—a gentle wind

gale—a very strong wind

global—something that happens throughout the world

jet stream—a fast-moving current of wind that blows from west to east around Earth

local—having to do with a small area

pollen—tiny grains that flowers produce

rustle—to move together and make a soft, crackling sound

wind turbine—an engine that is driven by propellers and uses energy from the wind to make electricity

Read More

Greene, Carol. *Please, Wind?* Rookie Ready to Learn. New York: Children's Press, 2011.

Sterling, Kristin. *It's Windy Today.* What's the Weather Like? Minneapolis: Lerner Publications Co., 2010.

Internet Sites

FactHound offers a safe, fun way to find Internet sites related to this book. All of the sites on FactHound have been researched by our staff.

Here's all you do:

Visit *www.facthound.com*

Type in this code: 9781429660549

Super-cool stuff! Check out projects, games and lots more at **www.capstonekids.com**

Index

Word Count: 165
Grade: 1
Early-Intervention Level: 17